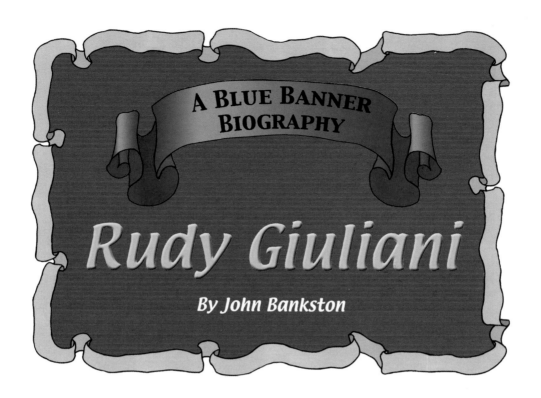

A BLUE BANNER
BIOGRAPHY

Rudy Giuliani

By John Bankston

Mitchell Lane
PUBLISHERS

P.O. Box 196
Hockessin, Delaware 19707
Visit us on the web: www.mitchelllane.com
Comments? email us: mitchelllane@mitchelllane.com

Printing   2   3   4   5   6   7   8   9

Blue Banner Biographies

Alicia Keys	Allen Iverson	Ashanti
Ashlee Simpson	Ashton Kutcher	Avril Lavigne
Beyoncé	Bow Wow	Britney Spears
Christina Aguilera	Christopher Paul Curtis	Clay Aiken
Condoleezza Rice	Daniel Radcliffe	Derek Jeter
Eminem	Eve	Ja Rule
Jay-Z	Jennifer Lopez	J.K. Rowling
Jodie Foster	Justin Berfield	Kate Hudson
Lance Armstrong	Lindsay Lohan	Mario
Mary-Kate and Ashley Olsen	Melissa Gilbert	Michael Jackson
Missy Elliott	Nelly	P. Diddy
Paris Hilton	Queen Latifah	Ritchie Valens
Rita Williams-Garcia	Ron Howard	**Rudy Giuliani**
Sally Field	Selena	Shirley Temple
Usher		

Library of Congress Cataloging-in-Publication Data
Bankston, John, 1974-
     Rudy Giuliani / John Bankston.
       p. cm. — (A blue banner biography)
Summary: A biography of the son of a convicted felon who grew up to become a tough prosecuting attorney and the mayor of New York City.
Includes bibliographical references and index.
     ISBN 1-58415-194-3
    1. Giuliani, Rudolph W. — Juvenile literature. 2. Mayors — New York (State) — New York — Biography — Juvenile literature. [1. Giuliani, Rudolph W. 2. Mayors.] I. Title. II. Series.
     F128.57.G58 B36 2003
     974.7'1043'092--dc21

2002153209

ABOUT THE AUTHOR: Born in Boston, Massachussetts, **John Bankston** began publishing articles in newspapers and magazines while still a teenager. Since then, he has written over two hundred articles, and contributed chapters to books such as *Crimes of Passion,* and *Death Row 2000,* which have been sold in bookstores across the world. He has written numerous biographies for young adults, including *Mandy Moore* and *Alexander Fleming and the Story of Penicillin* (Mitchell Lane). He currently lives in Portland, Oregon.

PHOTO CREDITS: Cover: AP Photo/Beth A. Keiser; p. 4 Getty Images; p. 8 Maiman Rick/Corbis Sygma; p. 11 Robert Maass/Corbis; p. 12 Hulton/Archive; p. 19 Franzo Adolfo/Corbis Sygma; p. 20 AP Photo/Richard Drew; p. 23 AP Photo/Mark D. Phillips; p. 24 AP Photo/Mark Lennihan; p. 27 Globe Photos, Inc.; p. 28 AP Photo/Doug Mills

CONTENTS

Despite his family background, Rudy went on to become the mayor of New York City.

Cops and Criminals

Harold Giuliani pointed the gun at the milkman's stomach and said, "You know what it is." The milkman did. Harold's partner-in-crime made off with a little over $100, but Harold was arrested while leaving the building. He would serve over a year in prison.

Harold was Rudy Giuliani's father. During the 2000 presidential race, both major candidates had fathers who'd been in politics. Al Gore's dad was a United States senator; George W. Bush's father was the 41st president. At the same time, the mayor of the largest city in the United States had a very different family history. His father wasn't a senator or a president. He was a convicted felon.

Yet in spite of his family's background, Rudy not only became the mayor of New York City, but also helped convict both crooked cops and corrupt politicians as a young lawyer. He almost ran for senator. Many people still hope he'll some day become president. More than anything, Rudy proved family background doesn't have to end a dream.

After Harold's release from prison, he married Helen D'Avanzo, a woman he'd met at a party in 1929 and had been dating ever since.

Rudolph William Louis Giuliani was born in Brooklyn, one of the five boroughs of New York City. Rudy was born on May 28, 1944, less than ten years after his father got out of prison. He was Harold and Helen's first and only child. They had been trying to have a baby for a long time; Rudy was considered a miracle baby.

As a teen, Harold had been a boxer but poor eyesight kept him from winning matches. On the streets, he was a tough and successful fighter, swinging at anything he saw moving. He'd worked as a part-time plumber's assistant, but after Rudy was born he mainly did jobs for Leo D'Avanzo, Helen's brother. Harold worked as a bartender at Leo's restaurant, but also helped him in his other business. Leo was a loan shark. He loaned money to people illegally and charged them high interest rates.

> **Rudy's success has proven that family background doesn't have to end a dream.**

When they didn't pay him back, Harold used some of the skills he developed boxing.

Rudy didn't know much about his father's history or about the rest of the family. "I knew parts of it, but it was always a big secret and very shadowy," he admitted to *Time* magazine.

Those bad family influences were part of the reason the Giuliani family left Brooklyn when Rudy was seven. They moved to Garden City, a middle class town on Long Island. By then Rudy had been studying at the St. Francis of Assisi Roman Catholic Parochial School. Harold wanted his son raised in the Catholic faith, and he wanted him to get a good education. But what he mainly wanted was for Rudy to learn right from wrong. "My father compensated through me. In a very exaggerated way, he made sure I didn't repeat his mistakes in my life – which I thank him for, because it worked out," Rudy explained to *Time*. "He would say over and over, 'You can't take anything that's not yours. You can't steal. Never lie, never steal.' As a child and even as a young adult, I thought, what does he keep doing this for? I'm never going to steal anything."

Rudy's father wanted his son raised in the Catholic faith, and he wanted him to get a good education.

Rudy's family's connection to crime, however, wasn't only on the wrong side of the law. Although both his uncle Leo and his son Lewis were criminals, four of Rudy's cousins were cops. While Lewis was a dangerous car thief who was shot by FBI agents, Rudy's cousin Ralph Stanchi, Jr. was shot in the line of duty. A young man in Rudy's situation might have felt confused but Harold helped Rudy learn right from wrong.

Rudy did everything he could to live up to his father's expectations. After attending Long Island's St. Anne's, in the fall of 1957 he enrolled at the very selective Bishop Loughlin Memorial High School in Brooklyn. Mainly Irish and Italian American students went

Rudy Giuliani was an involved mayor, visiting Manhattan schools such as this one during his campaigns.

to Bishop Loughlin. The school had high standards. Most of its graduates went on to the best colleges in the country. But Rudy wasn't much of a student. One of Rudy's teachers, Jack O'Leary, told biographer Wayne Barrett, "I don't recall Rudy being on the honor roll. I would not think of him as in the top ten percent of that school."

Instead Rudy excelled at extracurricular activities, including baseball, prom committee, and the opera and catechism clubs. The catechism club provided training in Catholicism. At the time, Rudy was thinking about becoming a priest.

In his senior year, Rudy was campaign manager for George Schneider, one of the candidates for class president. Because of his work on Schneider's campaign, the students at Bishop Loughlin didn't vote him the "Most Likely to Succeed" or "Best Dressed." In the spring of 1961, Rudy Giuliani was voted "Class Politician."

His senior class didn't know how right they were.

> *Rudy wasn't much of a student. But instead of excelling at schoolwork, Rudy excelled at extracurricular activities.*

The Kennedy Legacy

For years, Harold Giuliani told anyone who would listen that someday his son was going to be the president of the United States. It might have sounded boastful, but by the fall of 1961 when Rudy enrolled at Manhattan College, it seemed like anything was possible.

The year before, the country had elected John F. Kennedy, the first Irish-Catholic president in the nation's history. Maybe Rudy could be the first *Italian*-Catholic president.

Manhattan College was an all-male Catholic College in the Bronx, another New York City borough. By then Rudy and his parents had moved to Bellmore, another town on Long Island. Rudy's day began very early in the morning when he took the Long Island Railroad to New York City. There he hopped on the subway and stayed on until the last stop – 242nd Street. Rudy had a demanding schedule, but he always worked hard. "Rudy was always very intense," his mother told Rudy's biographer Wayne Barrett. "It used to annoy me. Everything to him was real. It wasn't for fun… I used to say, 'Loosen up!'"

Rudy's intensity had some rewards. Most kids struggle in their first year at college, but Rudy actually did better than he'd done in high school. In his second year, he was elected class president and also became president of the Phi Ro Pi fraternity.

As much as Rudy liked President Kennedy, it was Kennedy's younger brother he truly admired. Robert Kennedy was attorney general. He was a lawyer who fought cases for the United States. He worked to end

When Rudy attended Manhattan College, he took the subway early in the morning. Rudy continued to ride the subway as mayor.

Robert Kennedy was Attorney General for the United States, and worked hard to fight organized crime. Kennedy's work inspired Rudy to apply to law school.

organized crime. In the 1960s, criminal organizations– sometimes called the mob or the mafia–were involved with a number of businesses, from legal ones like garbage collection to illegal ones like gambling. The criminal organizations used threats and violence to get what they wanted. For Bobby Kennedy, one of the most dangerous criminal organizations wasn't even a business but a labor union. Although unions are set up to help workers, the Teamsters Union had broken many laws.

Going after a powerful labor union was dangerous, but to Rudy it looked exciting.

By 1965, Rudy realized the priesthood wasn't for him. Rudy wanted to be a lawyer like Robert Kennedy.

When Rudy was accepted at New York University School of Law, the country was going through drastic changes. President Kennedy had been shot in Dallas, Texas, black people were participating in civil rights protests, and many young men were fighting in the Vietnam War. Few people understood the war and even fewer supported it.

While Rudy was in law school, many young men were fighting in the Vietnam War.

However, while many people his age were dying in Vietnam or protesting on college campuses, Rudy was studying. Many people were holding protests to show that they didn't like what was going on in America. Since he was in law school, Rudy didn't have to fight in the war. Rudy was careful because he knew getting arrested at an anti-war rally would destroy his dream of becoming a lawyer.

In 1968, Rudy graduated magna cum laude (an honor awarded to graduates with high grades) from New York University. His life was about to change. First he began working as a law clerk for Judge Lloyd F.

MacMahon, the chief judge of the Southern District of New York.

"Rudy was very intelligent and he had a great sense of humor," Judge MacMahon told Barrett. "He hadn't come up with a silver spoon in his mouth." The job didn't pay much, but Rudy got a lot of experience. He got good training and met many important people.

Rudy loved trying cases so much that he actually asked his coworkers to give him theirs.

Rudy also got married during this time. Regina Perruggi was a pretty young woman he'd known for a long time. In fact, he met her on one of his family's summer vacations to the Long Island shore. Regina was his second cousin. His mother wasn't concerned about Rudy dating a family member, but she didn't think they were right for each other. Despite his mother's concerns, Rudy and Regina got married in October of 1968.

Two years later, Rudy got his first chance to fight crime. He took a job as a prosecutor at the U.S. Attorney's Office. By this time, Robert Kennedy, like his brother, had died from a gunshot wound. To Rudy, carrying on Kennedy's work seemed like a dream come true.

Rudy loved trying cases. He actually went around the office asking his coworkers to give them one or two of theirs. He rarely got home before midnight and spent weekends working.

Rudy's job was to argue the government's side in criminal cases. He argued against all types of criminals who'd broken the law. When he won, the criminals – called defendants – usually went to jail. And Rudy hardly ever lost.

Once Rudy was trying a case and about to enter evidence when he noticed something un-usual. The lawyer for the defen-dant and the judge were both asleep!

"I didn't know what to do," he admitted in Barrett's biogra-phy, "so I decided the thing to do was to get very close to the de-fense lawyer and just yell that I wanted to put it into evidence. And I did. I yelled. I startled him. He awakened. The jury laughed." Rudy won the case.

In 1972, Rudy got another big break. A number of New York City police detectives had been accused of breaking the law. There were rumors they'd sold drugs, and taken money from criminals to ignore their crimes. The only way to convict the detectives was to use what was said in court.

In 1972, a number of New York City police detectives were accused of selling drugs and accepting bribes.

Bob Leuci was the only cop who would talk about what he did. It was Rudy's job to get Leuci ready for court. Rudy told him what types of questions he would be asked and made sure Leuci was being honest.

Unfortunately, Bob Leuci wasn't being honest. He lied about what he'd done, leaving out quite a few details. If those details came out in court, his testimony would be useless. But he was afraid to talk about everything. Rudy convinced him that was the only choice, offering him immunity (protection from being charged for anything he discussed in court).

Both a book and a movie came out about the court case Rudy had won. Across the country, people were talking about Rudy.

Leuci finally admitted to a list of crimes that filled 84 pages—everything from giving informants drugs to taking money from dealers. Because of Leuci's testimony, dozens of crooked cops went to jail.

A book and a movie both called *The Prince of the City* came out about the the court case. Across the country, people were talking about Rudy Giuliani.

Law and Order

*B*y 1975, Rudy Giuliani had earned a reputation as a tough prosecutor. In Washington, D.C., the Deputy Attorney General Harold R. Tyler knew of Rudy's work in New York and had heard good things about him from his former boss Judge Lloyd MacMahon. Tyler offered Rudy a job as an associate deputy attorney general. He'd also be Tyler's chief of staff, advising Tyler on important matters. Rudy took the job.

Working in Washington, D.C. was a dream come true for Rudy. Except that the president, Gerald Ford, was a Republican, and all of Rudy's heroes had been Democrats. But that didn't stop him. He registered as an Independent and went to work.

Rudy's job only lasted two years. Still, he learned a valuable lesson. As he explained in the biography *Rudy*, "Tyler was very good under pressure. I learned from him that in a pressure situation, the best thing to do was remain calmer than everybody else. I also learned that it was good to become angry and upset when everybody else is calm and complacent. It helps to motivate them."

Rudy's new job gave him more money than he'd ever earned, and he also began having more fun.

While Tyler may have been partially to blame for the bursts of temper Rudy later became famous for, he also helped him get his first job in private law practice.

In 1976, when Democrat Jimmy Carter won the presidential election, Gerald Ford was out of a job. So was Rudy.

Tyler approached some of the top private New York law firms and offered a package of five lawyers from the Justice Department, including Rudy and himself. With their reputation in government and the amazing contacts their government work had given them, many firms were interested.

There was only one problem. The partners at Patterson, Belknap, Webb, and Tyler didn't want to hire Rudy as a partner. Maybe it was his lack of an Ivy League education, maybe it was his relative youth. Rudy refused to take a job as an associate. Finally Patterson, Belknap, Webb, and Tyler hired Rudy as a partner.

Rudy is shown here in 1996 with his wife Donna, daughter Caroline and son Andrew.

Rudy's new job gave him a chance to make more money than he'd ever earned before. He also began having more fun. He was making new friends at the firm and staying out late. His marriage to Regina was falling apart. In fact, few of his co-workers even knew he was married. Regina and Rudy's marriage ended in 1982.

By 1987, Rudy Giuliani was making national headlines. Here, he announces the indictments of Wall Street executives for insider trading.

By then Republican Ronald Reagan had been elected president and Rudy was back in Washington, D.C., working as an associate attorney general. It was the third highest position in the Department of Justice. The job put him in charge of the Bureau of Corrections, the Drug Enforcement Agency and the U.S. Marshals. Although he only worked in the job for two years, it gave him a wealth of experience managing large departments.

On a trip to Miami during this time, Rudy met Donna Hanover, a local TV reporter. The two began dating. His relationship with Donna was a bit of happiness during a sad time in Rudy's life. His father had recently died from prostate cancer. In 1984, Donna and Rudy married. They would have two children – Andrew born in 1986 and Caroline in 1989.

In 1983, Rudy returned to New York City. He'd been hired as the U.S. Attorney for the Southern District of New York. This put him in charge of the federal prosecutions in New York City and the surrounding areas. He worked hard to arrest drug dealers and mobsters. He went after corrupt government officials and stockbrokers. Rudy's name was often associated with high profile trials, his picture was on the front page of newspapers, and he was interviewed on television. During a period when the crime rate in New York City kept going up, Rudy was trying to do something about it. From 1983 to 1989, Rudy's office boasted 4,152 criminal convictions. Only twenty-five of those were ever reversed on appeal.

Rudy's name was often associated with high profile trials and his picture was on the front page of newspapers.

Yet even as he labored to put criminals in jail, Rudy realized that there were still many things terribly wrong with the city he loved. He wanted to do more to improve the city.

The Rotten Apple

*A*n illegal drug called crack cocaine came to America in the 1980s. Cheap and highly addictive, the drug helped fuel a steady increase in violent crime across the country. Since the 1970s, New York's mental hospitals had been releasing a steady stream of patients. Many of them wound up living on the streets of New York. A few were associated with horrible crimes.

By 1990, there were almost one million New Yorkers on welfare – the highest number since the Great Depression. 131 of the Fortune 500 companies were based in New York City. By 1990, over 100 of them had left. According to *Time* magazine, 59% of New Yorkers wished they could also leave the city.

Worse than the companies leaving, worse than the homelessness, even worse than the rising crime rate, to many residents the worst thing was their overall lack of hope.

Rudy refused to give up. He realized it was time for him to do more than just prosecute criminals. It was time to run the city. It was time for him to run for mayor. Rudy told the press, "Now is the time to take back our city from the violent criminals on our streets and the white collar criminals in their office suites, from the drug dealers in abandoned buildings and the crooked politicians who have abandoned their oath of office. It is time to restore the reputation of New York, so that again our city will be known for its libraries, its universities, its culture, its industry and its spirit – not as it is known today for crime, crack and corruption."

Rudy visits the Bronx during his 1989 mayoral campaign.

It was May 17, 1989. He'd resigned from his job at the U.S. Attorney's Office and taken a job with a private firm. Rudy had vision and ambition. What he didn't have was a seasoned organization. Most of the people working on the Guiliani for Mayor campaign were his friends – none of them had worked in politics. On top of that, Rudy was a Republican. New Yorkers hadn't elected a Republican mayor in over two decades.

Rudy lost to David Dinkins by the narrowest margin in the history of New York elections. But Rudy didn't give up. He studied his mistakes and put together a group to help him win the next election. In his second attempt, Rudy was elected mayor of New York City on November 2, 1993.

Rudy celebrates his 1993 election as New York City Mayor with wife Donna and son Andrew (lower-right).

Rudy had a difficult job ahead of him, but he was up to the challenge. He followed the broken window theory, which says if a window is broken in a building and left unrepaired, more broken windows will follow. Rudy believed this could be applied to smaller crimes – if they were ignored, worse crimes would follow.

Rudy had the police arrest people for crimes big and small. Panhandlers and the homeless were directed to shelters. Over 600,000 New Yorkers were taken off welfare.

Rudy's focus on smaller crimes seemed to work. Overall crime dropped by 57% and murder by 65%. For five years in a row, the F.B.I. named New York the safest large city in America. Rudy was very popular. When he ran for re-election in 1997, he easily defeated Ruth Messinger, winning four out of five New York City boroughs. But Rudy's popularity wouldn't last forever.

Rudy had the police arrest people for crimes big and small. Crime dropped, and Rudy became very popular.

America's Mayor

By the fall of 2001, many New Yorkers were tired of Rudy Giuliani. There had been a number of cases of police violence that tarnished the image of law enforcement in New York. Many people were also upset that Rudy fined impolite cab drivers and car alarm owners in an effort to increase the city's hospitality. People thought Rudy was being too tough. Some people did not like Rudy's personal life either. He was regularly seen in public dating Judith Nathan while still married to Donna Hanover and he'd moved out of Gracie Mansion, living with two other men in a New York apartment. Rudy's job approval rating had fallen to 32%.

Rudy's bid for the United States Senate ended when he was diagnosed with prostate cancer – the same disease that had killed his father. His battle with it left him weak and tired. New Yorkers were ready for him to retire, and he was ready to go.

September 11, 2001 dawned as just another New York City morning. It was bright and sunny as commuters packed subways and cab drivers made their way along the city streets. Stockbrokers and other business people made their way to the World Trade Center on Wall Street, the financial center of New York.

But September 11 wasn't just another day for New Yorkers — or for anyone in America.

Hijackers had taken over the controls of four airplanes. They crashed one of the planes into the Pentagon, a government building in Washington, D.C. Another crashed into a Pennsylvania field. Courageous passengers stopped that plane from reaching Washington, D.C.

Before Rudy was diagnosed with prostate cancer, he was planning to run against Hillary Clinton (left) for the United States Senate.

Rudy, President Bush (center) and New York Fire Commissioner Thomas Van Essen (right) observe the damage to the World Trade Center on September 14, 2001.

The two other planes hit the twin towers of the World Trade Center. Rudy arrived at the World Trade Center just after the second tower was hit. He moved into the Office of Emergency Management center near the towers. When the south tower collapsed, Rudy was almost trapped inside.

Rudy came close to losing his life. In the collapse of the towers, over 3,000 New Yorkers lost their lives, including 343 firefighters and 23 police officers. In the horrible aftermath, Rudy told America that the "number of casualties will be more than any of us can bear." He was right. But in the days that followed, he reminded New Yorkers and all Americans that thanks to the bravery of the firefighters and police officers, more than 20,000 lives were saved.

"Tomorrow New York is going to be here," Rudy said on September 11th. "And we're going to rebuild and we're going to be stronger than we were before... I want the people of New York to be an example to the rest of the country, and the rest of the world, that terrorism can't stop us."

Rudy's courage and strength provided inspiration to the survivors. He went to dozens of funerals and coordinated the incredible clean-up effort at the site of the destroyed towers. When he left office in January of 2002, many wondered if someday he would run for president. Since then Rudy has given lectures and focused on writing a book. The book, called *Leadership*, was published in October 2002. He and Donna Hanover divorced in July of 2002. In May of 2003, he married Judith Nathan. Although Rudy isn't certain what the future holds for him, he has this to say about the future of America, "We're not in a different world," Rudy explained to *Time* magazine. "It's the same world as before, except now we understand it better. The threat and the danger were there, but now we recognize it. So it's probably a safer world now."

> *Rudy's courage and strength after the World Trade Centers were hit provided inspiration to the survivors.*

CHRONOLOGY

1944 Rudolph William Louis Giuliani is born on May 28th in Brooklyn, New York

1951 family moves from Brooklyn to Garden City, a suburb on Long Island, New York

1957 begins attending Bishop Loughlin Memorial High School in Brooklyn

1961 voted "class politician;" graduates high school; enrolls at Manhattan College, a Catholic University in the Bronx

1965 graduates from Manhattan College; accepted by New York University School of Law

1968 graduates from New York University; begins working as a clerk for Judge Lloyd F. MacMahon; marries Regina Peruggi

1970 begins working at the U.S. Attorney's Office

1973 named chief of Narcotics Unit at the U.S. Department of Justice

1975 named associate deputy attorney general

1977 begins working in a private law practice

1981 President Ronald Reagan nominates Rudy associate attorney general

1982 marriage to Regina is annulled

1983 becomes U.S. Attorney for Southern District of New York

1984 marries Donna Ann Kofnovec Hanover

1986 son Andrew Harold is born

1989 resigns as U.S. attorney and begins working for the law firm of White and Case; daughter Caroline is born; loses mayor's race to David Dinkins

1993 wins mayor's race

1997 wins reelection

2001 terrorists destroy New York's World Trade Center

2002 *Leadership* is published

2003 marries Judith Nathan

FOR FURTHER READING

Burby, Liza N. *A Day in the Life of a Mayor: Featuring New York City Mayor Rudy Giuliani.* New York: Powerkids Press, 2001.

Lovett, Sarah. *Kidding Around New York City: A Young Person's Guide.* Santa Fe, NM: John Muir Publications, 1993.

Wheeler, Jill C. *September 11, 2001: The Day That Changed America.* Minneapolis: Abdo & Daughters, 2002.

On the Web:

Archives of 107th Mayor Rudolph Giuliani
    http://home.nyc.gov/html/rwg/home.html

Who2 Profile: Rudolph Giuliani
    http://www.who2.com/rudolphgiuliani.html

Time's 2001 Person of the Year: Rudy Giuliani
    http://www.time.com/time/poy2001/

INDEX